MW00783373

LARGE PRINT
UNDER THE SEA

EASY COLOR & FRAME

new seasons®
a division of Publications International, Ltd.

New Seasons is a registered trademark of Publications International, Ltd.

Copyright © 2021 Publications International, Ltd. All rights reserved.
This book may not be reproduced or quoted in whole or in part by any
means whatsoever without written permission from:

Louis Weber, CEO
Publications International, Ltd.
8140 Lehigh Ave
Morton Grove, IL 60053

Images from Shutterstock.com

Permission is never granted for commercial purposes.

ISBN: 978-1-64558-685-2

Manufactured in China.

8 7 6 5 4 3 2 1

Let's get social!

 @Publications_International

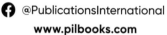 @PublicationsInternational

www.pilbooks.com